Rainbows of Hope

Photos and Poems by
Dwayne Cole

Parson's Porch Books

Rainbows of Hope
ISBN: Softcover 978-1-960326-38-6
Copyright © 2023 by Dwayne Cole

Parson's Porch Books is an imprint of Parson's Porch *&* Company (PP*&*C) in Cleveland, Tennessee. PP*&*C is a self-funded charity which earns money by publishing books of noted authors, representing all genres. Its face and voice is **David Russell Tullock** (dtullock@parsonsporch.com).

Parson's Porch *&* Company *turns books into bread & milk* by sharing its profits with the poor.

www.parsonsporch.com

Rainbows of Hope

Rainbows of Hope

Panpsychism

Rainbows of Hope open
windows of mystery and wonder,

calming our anxieties—
Inspiring our soul.

Painting scenes of heaven,
to illumine our earthly pathway.

Daniel Kantak Photo

Dedication

Sharing rainbow photos is a special act of friendship. This book is dedicated to Daniel Kantak my poet friend; and all who love rainbows. Daniel's photos and other shared photos are noted with names beneath the photos. All other photos are mine.

Walking in the rain
with a rainbow arching overhead.
Who can not be friends?

Preface

Photo by Daniel Kantak

Pan Words of Beauty and Wonder

"The teleology of the Universe is directed to the production of Beauty."
— Alfred North Whitehead

As I sit mindfully
starting to write my *Rainbows of Hope*,
I search for shining all inclusive words
to inspire—miraculous pan words.

My mind has a mind of its own.
It shouts pantheism, pan-en-theism,
pan-syncretism, panpsychism,
panexperientialism—

And the tv news shouts
the world inclusive,
bulldozing, fear creating word,
pandemic!

All the pan words
of this global age,
cry out to me!
Vying to be included!

Put down your mini-pad, grandad.
Slowly, a fire dance of beauty unfolds
and spreads, a fire dance of wonder.
A star dance of joy.

I am felled by shining beauty.
An all inclusive world soul—
A proto-consciousness
writes the poems for me.

Warmer than the rays of the smiling sun.
Subatomic particles flashing
as the rainbow dances—
Light of heaven—Pan-miracle.

Elfish star dust
swirling.

Gathering all pan words in tow.

Fire dance of wonder—
Lighting poetry's flame!

Glorious Rainbows of Hope!

Introduction

To speak of glorious rainbows of hope wrapped in a covenant of kindness is not a denial of the destructive power of floods. Nature is sometimes caught without its halo. In 1999 alone, 35,000 people died from floods, the worst being in Venezuela.

There is a deep mystery to the life/death/rebirth cycle that is not easily explained. My poetry of ecology seeks to unite science and the humanities in one clear voice to speak of this mystery. This poetic panpsychist approach sees our life as one with the world soul. The world soul moves toward Truth, Beauty, Goodness, Art, Adventure, and Peace, all the values of civilization at its best. Poetry speaks of this adventurous mystery, often holding paradoxical ideas in tension, without the need to explain them. Poetry begins in wonder and mystery.

When poetry does its best, the wonder and mystery remain.

The eye of God
The all encompassing circle
Showing love for all

One purpose of these rainbow poems is to instill Beauty, Wonder, Kindness, and Hope in our daily lives. The magical composition of rainbows is Beauty wrapped in Mystery, as if an enchanter waved a wand. God is the Enchanting Poet of the world; and the rainbow, uniting heaven and earth, is poetry that bears the mark of the Eternal.

As you see these Rainbows of Hope—

> Like Anne of Green Gables
> Find your place in Rainbow Valley,
> a place to dream.
> Let nature become your friend,
> teach you how to play and love.

*****

> Rainbows unweave storm clouds.
> Empty the haunted darkness.
>
> Rainbows add the shine of heaven
> on evil filled dark days.
>
> When rainclouds are scattered
> glory is shed for our pathway.

When I send clouds over the earth, and a rainbow appears in the sky, I will remember my promise to you and to all other living creatures.
Never again will I let floodwaters destroy all life. When I see
the rainbow in the sky, I will always remember the promise that I have made to every living creature.—Genesis 9:12-13

This rainbow promise was given to Noah and his descendants after the great flood.

How quickly it glows
How quickly it dims
Life is a rainbow

*****

To see the Infinite
Look at the glowing sky
Rainbow of Hope

D. Cole

In the Bible there are three rainbows after the one in Genesis
9:12-13. In Ezekiel 1:28, after Ezekiel sees a vision of God, he says, "I was
surrounded by a bright light. as colorful as a rainbow that appears after a
storm. I realized that I was seeing the brightness of the Lord's glory!"
(Ezekiel 1:28).

John, on the Island of Patmos, sees "a rainbow (iris) with bright colors of rubies and emeralds that transforms trees and mountains into heaven's glow. (Based on Revelation 4:1-3)

John sees another vision of "an angel coming down from heaven, clothed with a cloud. And a rainbow (iris) was on his head, his face was like the sun, and his feet like pillars of fire" (Revelation 10:1).

In using jasper, carnelian, and emerald, gems of various colors, to describe the rainbow, the writer of Revelation is showing how precious the rainbow is to God's people.

Jasper was known as a nurturing color that brought support, tranquility, and wholeness in times of stress. Jasper was believed to provide protection and absorb negative energy.

Carnelian is a reddish brown color associated with energy and creativity. By infusing light this gem brought power to prevent misfortune.

The rainbow around the throne of God is also described as emerald in color. The circular green rainbow around the throne of God signifies that God is a covenant keeping God whose promises will be fulfilled. In the Christian tradition emerald was used to describe Christ as purity, kindness, and goodness. (See Appendices II and III for key biblical verses that show how God's relational kindness and Jesus' kindness fulfill rainbow promises).

God smiled—
The rainbow appeared.
God is with us.

Pam Roseveare Photo

The Eye of God

God, the Poet of wonder,
paints a rainbow circle
around the whole world to say—
I am in the world and for the world.
In you and for you.

Rainbows in Myth

In ancient Greek mythology, Iris/Isis, is the goddess of rainbows. This goddess was a messenger between heaven and earth, representing how the rainbow bridges the two. In Homer's epic, the Iliad, Iris was a winged creature who specifically served as the messenger of Zeus.

For as long as there have been rainbows, there have been dreamers and poets who have sought to bring hope in times of flooding disasters. What's behind these dreams? The closer one gets to rainbows, the more elusive they are, which only adds to their legendary mystique. Rainbow myths have become a part of many cultures. The various legends of rainbows from different parts of the world are a testament to the fascination of this meteorological magic. When rainbows speak, I will listen.

Legends about rainbows usually take on mythic character. This does not mean that these myths are completely free of truth.

Legends and myths often start with curious dreamers—men and women who were captivated by the event they were witnessing but couldn't explain. The closer they tried to get to rainbows, the more unattainable they became. These distant bursts of beautiful light became the wonder of rainbow legends.

Shining As Rainbows

I spent much of my working life
hurrying from one ministry
to another, from nursing homes
to hospital visits—to pray with the ill.

Now retired in Alaska,
I walk under trees
illumined by rainbows.
I do not hurry. I bow often.

I contemplate
until l am a leaf on
a rainbow glistening tree
trembling just above me.

The shining leaves
whisper—
See how the rainbow
illumines us!

Let the light
fall on you.
Sit and stay awhile—
heaven is all around.

Illness, pain, and death
are not as you think.
Our leaves fall to the ground.
New ones come back to astound.

I feel goodness,
grace,
and love,
Shining all around.

I do not hurry.
I bow often.
I walk on to shine
in the world—

A rainbow
of promise, security,
and hope!

D. Cole

I have climbed mountains
wrapped in Easter egg rainbows,
with Angel harps playing.
I joined the music praying—
Let my life be a rainbow!

This is my prayer
Rainbows to warm our soul
Warmth to share

Daniel Kantak Photo

My Rainbows of Hope

Muse, overwhelm me
Let me behold your glory
Angels singing
Rainbow promises of hope
Held secure in friendships

From antiquity,
Unchanged for millions of years.

Genetically coded,
shapeshifters of magic.

Uplifting and challenging—
Rainbow colors shine from heaven.

(See my book, *Dragonfly Magic*, listed on line at Parson's Porch Books,
Barnes & Noble, and Amazon)

Daniel Kantak Photo

With heaven's colors,
rainbows paint God's apology
for angry skies.

*****

There is nothing
More beautiful than a rainbow
After gentle rain

You are chosen
because of
God's
wonderful kindness.
(Gal. 1:6, CEV)

D. Cole

We are chosen
To be God's kindness rainbow
Transforming the world

It's hard to know where
rainbow ends and tundra begins.
Life is a rainbow.

Be Still

When I am silent
I find rainbows waiting
to thrill my soul.

Rainbows of Hope

I have great faith
in the goodness of life—
Rainbows from heaven.

Faith in deep yearnings
of the soul rising higher—
Will be fulfilled.

Faith in dreams
awaiting realization.
Challenges fill sky.

Take the colors
at the edge of rainbows.
Paint new dreams!

Hope shines on the horizon!

Sometimes the whole
world is a rainbow
drawing all into its
radiance.
Let it shine!
Let it shine!

D. Cole

Celestial Rainbows

Whole world is sometimes—
A rainbow painted with
Angel wings.

I wish I could paint for you a rainbow
Splashed with all the colors of heaven.
And hang it in the window of your soul.

So each new day would radiate
love energy from the rainbow
opening new dimensions of
promise, security, and hope.

But that is God's wondrous work!
Gift from the celestial realm!
(This poem was inspired by Ann Weems,
Reaching for Rainbows)

Like Anne of Green Gables
find our place in Rainbow Valley.
Perfect place to dream.
Let nature become our friend,
teach us how to play and love.

Dwayne Cole

I look at the blue sky
Through deep blue feathery eyes.
Every shade is there—
Bright radiant day dreaming skies,
dark stormy nightmare skies.

Steller's jay blue sway
Tweet your territorial tune
Chase my blues away
Dark Delta variant clouds
Rainbow radiant promise

God and Evil:

An Ode to Kindness

Dwayne Cole

Seeing rainbows
The soul is enraptured
We believe and trust
God's care for us

I used this rainbow photo as the cover to my book,
God and Evil: An Ode to Kindness.
This book will help you maintain hope
in these troubling pandemic days.
Living with unanswered questions.

Evil is not a puzzle to be solved;
it is a mystery in which we live.

I share this story, climaxing with a rainbow, from that book, as an example of hope in
troubling times.

Wendell was my best friend from the time we entered the first grade in
school. We did all the things boys typically did growing up in the rural
South in the post- depression decades of the forties and fifties. On the
school grounds we played marbles and the daring game of follow the leader,
which took us on adventures through the surrounding woods. In high
school we played baseball and football. Wendell was a big guard in football,
and he was good enough to consider a college and pro career. I was a lean
and mean right end playing on both the offensive and defensive teams and
lucky to be injury free after four years of tackling and being tackled. After
canning his opposing guard, Wendell would make sure my lane stayed open
on short pass plays. In fact, he could be one of the reasons I survived
largely unscathed.

Then it happened. Just two weeks before graduation, Wendell was killed
when two cars collided head-on at a curve in the road. His older brother,
who was driving drunk, was injured but fully recovered, at least physically.
The two elderly people in the other car, who were outstanding citizens and
active church members, were both also killed instantly. When I learned of
the accident, I was stunned and filled with grief.

I remember going home from the funeral and climbing on the old Allis
Chalmers farm tractor to cultivate the fields. I wanted to
be alone with my troubling thoughts, undisturbed. Soon a thunderstorm
began to form and the sky darkened,
as though nature was in sympathy with my dark mood.
Lightning flashed and thunder rolled. I cried out
in the spirit of Job, shaking my fist at the heavens,

Why, O God,
did Wendell die
in this terrible car collision?

Why do you make
and then break
such a strong youth?
Did you really need another flower in heaven,
as the preacher said?

No answer came.
The clouds were not rolled back,
and there was no voice from heaven.
But the storm passed on. The gentle rain came
and washed away my tears. As the tractor rumbled on,
I had a deep feeling of God's presence.

A sparkling rainbow appeared on the horizon,
and I found strength and hope in the glow of the rainbow
to go on with my life.

A Rainbow Poem,
Please be still and listen—
God is speaking!

Dwayne Cole

Photos are poems
Poems are photos
Be still and listen

Dragonfly Photos by my Florida friend, G. W. Reid,
Who has now gained his angel wings in Heaven.

Nature's Dragonfly Miracles

Two hundred million years

genetically coded

rainbows of color.

This laggard species

dries in the sun a few hours

and lifts into flight.

Waving its wings.

Art pages flapping in sun.

Rainbow Beauty
to behold.

Wonder unfolds!

Nature Speaks

Ripples in the stream
whisper messages as the water flows
over stones and around larger rocks.

Red, silver, and pink salmon
are attuned to the soft music,
streaming flashes of rainbows.

I stand in awe of their patience.
Soothed by the soft music.
Heart pounding with gratitude!

Thank you, Thank you
for teaching me to be still and
receive the gift of inner peace.

*****

Silvery smolts
Flashing rainbows of color
Beauty to behold

You can't pull a name out of a hat
to name a special cat.

And one name will not do.
You need at least two.

Lady Gray,
crossed the Rainbow Bridge.

Grace filled for 15 years.
Now free to climb sun rays.

Leap from moon beams
to twinkling stars.

And when you need a hug
Look for me, Lady Gray,

sliding down rainbows—
bringing the light of heaven.

On your dark days,
walk with me into eternity's light!

(Written for my friend, Bill Johnson,
upon the death of his pet cat)

Daniel Kantak Photo

Oh uncontrollable light
Heaven's rainbow so luminous
Transforming the world
Showing way to live in beauty
Filled with wonder and awe

Photo by Paxton Thomas

Alaska's horizons
Wrapped in promise, security, hope
Beauty unfolds

(See my sermon "A Rainbow of Promise, Security, and Hope"
in my book, *Jesus' Transforming Gentle Teachings*. A condensed version of the
sermon can be seen in appendix I at the end of this book.)

Daniel Kantak Photo

Rainbows of Hope

I have great faith
in kindness
Brought by rainbows

Faith in deep yearnings
of the soul
not yet fulfilled

See rainbows
Slow down
Take off shoes

Listen
Remember
Forgive

Breathe deep
Recover from fears
Heal

Hope
Wrapped
in goodness

Life can be a storm
Your hope is a rainbow
Family is the gold.

Kindness Rainbow

God's rainbow promises
are expressions of kindness
that heal head stress
and heart strain.

My Big Idea—

My big idea is kindness.
If I had a bullhorn
I would sound kindness
from the mountain tops of Alaska
to the tip of Florida's most Southern shore.

Kindness among
all my brothers and sisters,
especially all my family in Georgia.
Every person is precious,
every one has value.

What is your big idea?
In America we can do anything!
Especially, become a kindness rainbow!
Right!!!

From Fear To Love

Out of the storm clouds of fear
Comes shining radiance

Drape your ribbons of light
As garlands around our neck

Our hearts welcome your presence
Leaping toward your sustaining Grace

The rising rainbow a flowing stream
A dervish glamour dance

What could We do
But take you in our embrace

Crying you are our
Love miracle

Rainbow of wonder
Radiance of joy

Let me be an instrument
Of your radiant love

This little light of mine
I'm going to let it shine

Be silent and let the rainbow
Finish the song

I walked into a beautiful rainbow.
Faced the deep fears of pandemic.

Felt I was not of this time and place.
Gazed and waited.

Then Nature's Beauty looked back at me.
I became one with the visible universe.

One with heaven's blue canopy over me.
Security, Promise, and Hope within me.

Ascended into higher realms unknown.
Awakened by Beauty and Grace.

Emboldened by nature's tender touch—
The strength of Oneness!

Began to see with new eyes—
All my fears and pain were drawn into the heart of
Kindness.

Overcome with Goodness and Mercy!

The unbounded Joy
of being kissed by a Lover—
Dancing in a new day.

Finding one's name written
in the shining clouds.

The gift is buried treasure.
Hope in Beauty and Wonder!

A Tribute to My Brother, Herbert

I just read the tribute Randy and Ricky
Wrote about their daddy, my oldest brother.

My soul was weeping
and laughing with gratitude!

This little man
with a big heart of love

stood tall
in our family.

He was the sunlight in our days
and the twinkling star in our night.

The rainbow of promise
comfort and hope in our storms.

One day with mother and daddy
and all our heavenly family,

we will hear the message,
"Beloved, Welcome home!"

Mountain Colored Easter Egg

Gaze with soul shining
Discover beauty of grace
Find the prize
A hymn of victory
An image of resurrection wonder!

A Prayer of Blessing
Blessing

As You Go---
Remember This

Dwayne Cole

God's goodness shines as bright as the rising sun.

As you go, please remember this—

It is by the goodness of God that we are born

into this world in the first place.

And it is by the grace of God that we are held

every step we take in life.

It is by the love of God revealed in the life, death,

and resurrection of Jesus

that we are being redeemed. Amen

(I used the prayer above as the benediction in
worship for most of my ministry. The book
pictured is a sermonic commentary on the prayer.)

Become a Rainbow

Night time spooky dreams
Fears grip like the jaws of a vise
and won't let go
Tossing and turning fretfully
Dawn brings warm sunshine

Go and find a place
to rest in the beauty of the sunrise
Feel the colors from the edge of rainbows
bathing your soul
with grace and goodness

Lifted into the presence of alpenglow clouds
Aglow with the life-giving sun
Come alive in the radiance
Rest in the grace of the new day
Be free from all anxiety

Become what you never dreamed
For the first time
Burst into new life
Full of freshness and vitality
Now and forever

Rainbows Turn Trees Magical

My six brothers, six sisters, and I grew up loving trees.
Three brothers and four sisters have died. I often think of them
residing now in heaven along with mother and daddy.

When Herbert and C. E. were teens,
they especially liked trees. They got the idea
to tie an old iron framed bed high in a walnut tree.

After a hard morning of plowing mules in corn rows, they
would eat a quick lunch, climb in the walnut tree.
They would tip their hat, take a bow, and lie down for a nap.

Seeing this tree and mountain wrapped in a rainbow
I took a bow, and said, "Thank you, brothers and sisters, mother
and daddy, for visiting me."

Were they in the rainbow glistening tree top?
If elves dwell in trees and angels descend on Jacob's ladder, my
family can slide down heaven's rainbow and sit a spell.

I know this: Seeing this tree aglow
with shimmering incandescence, wrapped in a rainbow, I sure
felt their presence!

The more I see rainbows
The more I love them
As God's art shows

Love and acceptance of all persons without regard for race, gender, or religion is the fruit of kindness.

Dwayne Cole

I use this rainbow/photo/poem to inspire me as an ally of LGBTQ+ and all who suffer from prejudice.

Denali

Out of the low drifting clouds
a rainbow appears,
followed by mountains
walking to and fro.
Cleansed by the showers.
Off in the heavens, Denali,
the highest peak in North America,
lifts the cloud veil, and winks
like a courting lover.

D. Cole

D. Cole

Denali

In the foothills of Denali

Painted with autumnal colors

Crowned with a rainbow of hope

Grizzly mom and cubs

Grazing on ripe blueberries

Russet birch trees rise

Ground squirrels eating seeds

Gurgling glacier fed stream

Singing a cheerful song

As it flows along to sea

If eyes are for seeing

Beauty needs no other reason

For being

D. Cole

I woke at 10:30 p.m.
with ribbons of rainbow on my pillow.
Heard the leaves whispering, "Be still.
An art show is in progress."

I became one with the leaves
quivering on the edge of the rainbow.
Awash in the pastel colors
of the Great Artist's palette.

After an hour of photo capturing
the changing hues of red, pink,
purple, yellow, bronze,
silver and gold—

All melding into
one grand art scene.
All more valuable than
money in the bank!

Deeply enriched,
I fell back asleep.
Secure in dreams
of heavenly peace!

The rainbow is God's promise—
I will always be kind to you.
(Based on Isaiah 54:9-10, CEV)

D. Cole

I have great faith
in the goodness of life
brought by angels of mercy
from heaven above.

Faith in songs not yet composed,
in poems not yet penned, and
in deep yearnings of the soul
not yet fulfilled.

In my ministry of 50+ years
I planted heaven's seeds
of challenge and hope.

My gentle teachings
are but a dream awaiting realization,
a challenge I still strive to meet.

If this seems grandiose, forgive me.

I desire the stream of life
to overflow with

    goodness,
        grace
           and love.

All be guided by rainbows of

promise,

security,

and hope.

Of this I am sure—
My faith is secure
in rainbows.

(LGBTQ+ Flag—In 1978, the artist Gilbert Baker, an openly gay man designed the first rainbow flag as a symbol of pride for the LGBTQ+ community. Baker saw flags as the most powerful symbol of pride. He saw the rainbow as a natural flag from the sky, so he adopted the colors of the rainbow for the stripes of his flag—red for life, orange for healing, yellow for sunlight, green for nature, turquoise for art, indigo for harmony, and violet for spirit.

By 1994, the rainbow flag was established as the symbol for LGBTQ+ pride, and it became an international symbol.
As an ally, I use it in my poetry.)

I woke at 10:56 p. m.
in Anchorage, Alaska,
and witnessed
God, the Great Artist,
Mounting an Art Show.

I did not know
if I were dreaming—
Witnessing the visible heavens,
Or the invisible center
of everything.

The bright green
cottonwood leaves
were trembling like my soul.
The landscape shining
like a snapshot of the first creation.

A rainbow dipped down
through the clouds.
Licking the ice crystals,
nuzzling the tree leaves,
and painting the Chugachs
like they were giant Easter eggs.

All the shimmering colors of the rainbow
caressed my soul.
Glory to God in the Heavens!

Heaven and earth became
a rainbow of colors!
The birch trees dressed
in golden britches
danced together
becoming a field of fire,
a cauldron of gold!

The whole sky and mountains
became an artist's palette of rainbow hues—
From one bright vista to another.
Vanishing edges of heaven
and earth merge together as one.

The moon, not wanting
to be left out of the art show,
began to peep through
the garden of leaves
and purple clouds
precisely at midnight.

In just five short hours
the sun will rise again in the East
brazen and bright,
giving new life and energy
to all living things.

Baptized in holy sensual light,
I fell asleep in the realm
where time ceases,
in the glow of rainbows
and moon beams—
All demons painted into
a corner.

So may it be!
So may a new day dawn
with heaven's glorious light
and all sing together
in our transformed world!

Do Not Hurry

Bow often.
Walk on to shine
in the world—

A rainbow
of promise,
security,
and hope!

D. Cole

Dragonfly photos by G.W. Reid

Dragonfly: Art Pages Flapping

Unchanged for
two hundred million years.

Genetically coded rainbows of color
emerge from dark gray water nymph.

Dry in the sun a few hours
and burst into flight!

Laggard Dragonflies

Unchanged for
two hundred million years.

Genetically coded rainbows of color.

Dry in the sun a few hours
and flutter into flight!

D. Cole

Storms

Monster storms pound
Trees bend to ground

Nature on rampage
Caught without angel wings

God in Heaven
looks the other way

Zip your raincoat good
Pull up the hood

Like Job bend
into the wind

Rainbow
Appears

Upside Down Rainbow

An upside down rainbow
is a frown turned into a smile.

It's a little off kilter,
Maybe a wry smile,
filled with intrigue.

Causing me to think,
What is God up to?

The rainbow is a symbol
of promise, security, and hope.

I wish I could paint for you
a rainbow and hang it like a halo
in the window of your soul.

So that you could begin each day
with God smiling on you.

Ali storm clouds jab
Ocean surges forth
Rainbow all aglow

Dark storm clouds pound
Ocean pours down in buckets
Rainbow hope appears

Rainbows are God's hand
writing divine messages
of promise and hope.

Rest secure in peace.

God gives rainbows of promise, security, and hope.

A Golden Heaven Sings Psalms of Praise!

Prophets of Doom,

sound the trumpet call.

Our history reveals wars

and bombs that have blown

the doors of hell off their hinges.

Demons of hate walk to and fro

across our land. Our air is polluted

and our rivers are poisoned.

Prophets of hope—

Wake us from our slumber!

It is time to rise!

Climb the mountain of glory.

Loving kindness opens the doors of heaven

and new eyes open to the Glory of God.

"Try to be a rainbow in someone's cloud"
                    —Maya Angelou

D. Cole

Sometimes you can hear drum beats—
A symphony inside a storm.

A Vivaldi violin plays—
God the Poet of the universe.

Zestful music to our soul—
A rainbow of glorious hope.

*****

God the Poet of nature,
Tenderly caring for children.

Riding high on the rainbow
of promise, security, hope.

Bridging heaven and earth
with the gift of Peace, Sweet Peace!

*****

When storm clouds gather
And rain sends floods on the earth
Become a rainbow

*****

There is nothing
More beautiful than a rainbow
After gentle rain

rest in peace youngest brother
the illusion of this world drained
from your eyes --now you see
with pure vision
of spirit/soul.

Good night Jimmy, see you when I awaken
when my time comes.—Daniel Kantak

(The rainbow, bridging heaven and earth,
has always brought comfort in times of death. This photo was taken
and the poem was written by my friend, Daniel Kantak, upon the
death of his younger brother. Daniel is a published poet. You can see
more of his work in his book, *A Rumor About Shooting Stars.*)

Daniel Kantak Photo

Rainbows are special
in times of personal darkness
Rainbows bring healing

Conclusion

Lessons I learned from watching rainbows:

1). Rainbows are God's poems.

2). Watching rainbows contributes to keeping our body healthy, filled with the awesome adventure of youthfulness.

3). Watching rainbows can be a freeing and healing moment of letting go of anger and negative thoughts that gnaw away at the soul and replacing them with kind loving thoughts.

4). Mindfulness is important in staying centered. Do not let your mind dwell on past problems or future worries. Enjoy the awe and wonder of the present moment---the beauty of the rainbow skies, clouds, raindrops.

5). Centering on beauty is everything. Our thoughts and actions shape who we are.

6). Like a bride or groom marry yourself to the awesome beauty. Wedded to wonder—love, joy, and peace come to you like the sun splashed scenery around you.

7).Bridging heaven and earth, rainbows bring God's comfort in times of sorrow and grief.

8). There is nothing more beautiful than a rainbow after gentle rain.

Floods Worldwide

The flood story of the Bible is a Hebrew myth. Rainbow myths are a part of many cultures. In ancient Greek mythology, Iris/ Isis, is the goddess of rainbows. This goddess was a messenger between heaven and earth, representing how the rainbow bridges the two. In Homer's epic, the Iliad, Iris was a winged creature who specifically served as the messenger of Zeus.

For as long as there have been rainbows, there have been dreamers and poets who have sought to bring hope in times of flooding disasters. What's behind these dreams? The various legends of rainbows from different parts of the world are a testament to the fascination of this meteorological magic.

Floods are major disasters around the world. In 2020 alone, floods caused the death of more than six thousand people around the world. However, this death number is dwarfed in comparison to the peak recorded in 1999, when 35 thousand people died in floods, the deadliest being the one that hit Venezuela in December of that year.

While the death toll is the most critical impact of flooding incidents, it is not the only one. Floods leave many injured and homeless. Floods also bring massive economic damage by destroying buildings and infrastructure.

Floods impact our spiritual lives and our trust in God.

God's all encompassing love meets us in the midst of storms empowering us for kindness. The heart of the biblical message is that God is clothed in a covenant of faithful love. God's relational love is persuasive and luring, not coercive and controlling.

Instead of asking, Why does God not control flooding, we should ask why we are not controlling floods?
We have evolved with the power to conserve
and protect our environment.

As climate change causes global temperatures to rise, floods are expected to become more frequent and severe. A warmer atmosphere is able to retain more moisture, leading to an increase in intense downpours. It also affects snowmelt patterns. According to a 2022 report, the global population affected by flooding was expected to rise by 24 percent due to rising temperatures. With our scientific knowledge in hand, we know what is causing global warming. We know how to clean up the environment.

Let us all become rainbows of hope.

> Hope is a rainbow of many colors,
> painted across the skies.
>
> Wrapping heaven and earth as one—
> A ribbon at a time.
>
> There is nothing more beautiful
> than a rainbow after gentle rain.

Appendix I

A Rainbow of Promise, Security, and Hope

When I send clouds over the earth, and a rainbow appears in the
sky, I will remember my promise to you and to all other living
creatures. Never again will I let floodwaters destroy all life.
When I see the rainbow in the sky, I will always remember the
promise that I have made to every living creature.

—Genesis 9:`12-13

When you beg God for help, God will answer, "Here I am!"

Don't mistreat others or falsely accuse them or say something

cruel. Give your food to the hungry and care for the homeless.

Then your light will shine in the dark; your darkest hour will be

like the noonday sun.

—Isaiah 58:9-10

A Rainbow Over the Church

I wish I could paint for each or you a personal rainbow.

Splashed with all the colors of creation and hang it

in the window of your soul so that each new day w

would open with promise, security, and hope.

If I could I would wipe away your sorrow and pain,

and hold you close in comforting peace.

But God never promised that I could paint

a rainbow for you. That is God's splendid work.

I can only stand and gaze with you in awe and wonder.

Soon after I was called as pastor of Mount Sharon Cumberland Presbyterian Church, one day Beth, my wife, called me out to the backyard of the manse to look at a rainbow. It was splashed with all the colors of God and reached from one side of the sky to the other. It was as perfect as any rainbow we had ever seen. This one was special for it gave us the feeling that we had made the right decision in coming to minister with these good people. This rainbow, bridging heaven and earth, was like the signature of God, assuring that we were in the right place doing God's will. We were given the feeling of God's promise, security, and hope.

A Rainbow of Promise

The rainbow God gave to Noah and all people of God came after the great flood, as a promise wrapped in covenant love and kindness. The Bible is sacred to us today because we believe biblical promises are our promises. When God established the covenant, saying "I will be your God and you will be my people," we take that personally. We launch out and make new beginnings every day under that rainbow of promise. This promise is wrapped in the tender teachings of Jesus that have the power to transform our lives and heal a broken world. All tender teachings found in the religions of the world have this transforming power. Tenderness led Mother Theresa to pick up the abandoned children from the streets of Calcutta and bring them to the clinic for healing. Buddha said, my teaching is kindness. Our global age calls us to join hands with all who seek world transformation through tender teachings that say all life is precious and has value.

A Rainbow of Security

When we saw the rainbow over our Church, bridging heaven and earth, we had a deep feeling of security. Security comes as a gift from holding on to God's promises. The Poet of the world that painted the rainbow was moving our world a little closer to Beauty, Wonder, Goodness, and Peace. In our broken world, many are reaching for rainbows of security. Many are hungry and want to be fed, hurting and want solace. The crying want the angel wings that painted the rainbow to wipe their tears away. When dark days come, hold on to rainbow promises of security

A Rainbow of Hope

God's rainbows inspire hope. As God's people we are called to be rainbows of hope to the world. Isaiah, the great prophet in the Old Testament, is a proclaimer of hope. He wrote of "a bright new day" (Isaiah 58:9-10), like a garden that has plenty of rain, and like a spring that never goes dry.

Rainbow promises of hope are waiting to become reality as we become rainbows to each other and to our world. It gives me a great sense of peace to know that we are under the rainbow of promise, security and hope. (For a more complete version of this sermon see my book, *Jesus' Transforming Tender Teachings*, pages 219-224.)

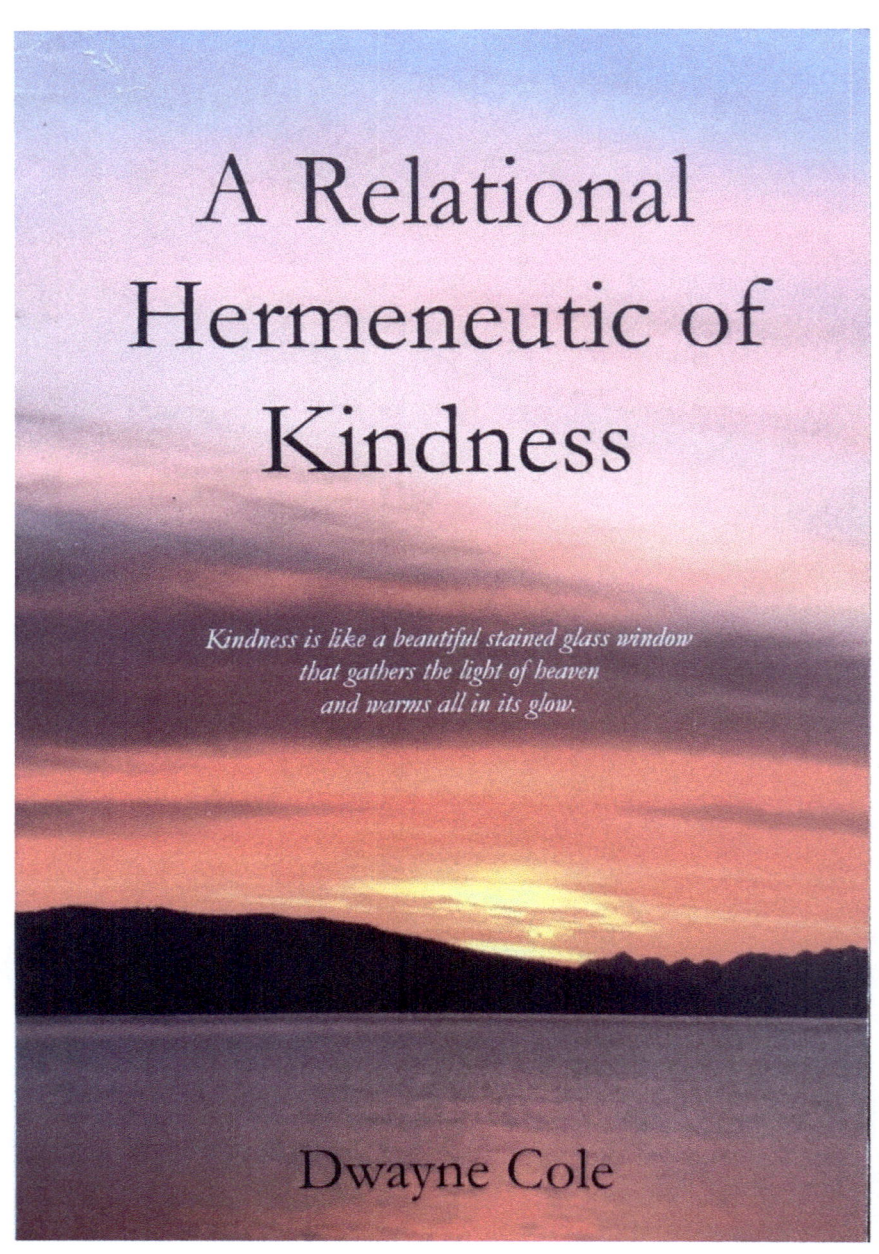

A Relational Hermeneutic of Kindness

*Kindness is like a beautiful stained glass window
that gathers the light of heaven
and warms all in its glow.*

Dwayne Cole

Appendix II: Rainbows Reveal God's Relational Kindness

Seeing God as relational kindness, is a lens through which I understand the Bible, and the best route for finding meaning in our lives and in our troubled world. A key biblical verse is—"God, you brought me safely through birth, and you protected me as a baby at my mother's breast. From the day I was born I have been in your tender care, and from my birth you have been by my side" (Author's paraphrase of Psalm 22:9-10).

Religions affirming faith in God have attempted to understand the nature of God and how God relates to the people of God and the world. In one sense God is beyond all human thoughts and wrapped in mystery. The biblical writers recognized this. Isaiah wrote that God's thoughts are not our thoughts and our ways are not God's ways (Isaiah 55:8-9). Expressing his thoughts about God, Paul said, "We see in a mirror dimly" and "We speak God's wisdom in a mystery." (1 Corinthians 13:12).

From the Bible, we know God revealed in the prophets, psalmists, and in Jesus as a uniquely personal and relational God, best described for me as creative responsive kindness. Responsive love is a phrase found often in process theology. Love is an often used word to describe God. Jesus' gentle teachings especially capture this central truth about God in the great commandment of love. I have chosen kindness as the best description of God for this reason: the word, love, has been so used and cheapened in our culture that it carries a lot of baggage. Love focuses for most people on emotion and not action. For this reason, I have chosen to simply say, God is kind. Kindness that is partial in us is all-embracing in God. As the creative impulse and adventurous energy that gives value to all of life, God is mystery. Yet God is present in the coming into being of all things. God calls all things into existence and tenderly guides and nurtures all things through the ages. The mystery of God has been seen in the magical beauty of rainbows.

The Psalms are best seen as joyful songs grounded in the goodness of God. This image of God's kindness is also found in the Old Testament prophets like Isaiah and Hosea. Isaiah's prayer is "Please, Lord, be kind to us! We depend on you. Make us strong each morning, and come to save us when we are in trouble." (Isaiah 33:2, CEV).

Here is Isaiah's answer to how God heard his prayer for kindness: Our God has said, encourage my people! Give them comfort. Speak kindly to Jerusalem and announce good news: Clear a path in the desert! Make a straight road for the Lord, our God is here! Just as shepherds care for their flocks, God will carry you in arms of compassion and gently lead you. (See Isaiah 40:1-11, CEV). Hosea speaks with the same tender image of God—

When Israel was a child, I loved him, and I called my son out of Egypt. I took Israel by the arm and taught them to walk. I led them with kindness and with love, not with ropes. I held them close to me. Like a mother I bent down to feed them (Author's paraphrase of Hosea 11:1-4).

In learning these sacred scriptures of his people, Jesus spiritually shook hands with Isaiah and Hosea. He daily shaped his ministry from the suffering servant songs in Isaiah and the tender story and example of Hosea. In Jesus' gentle teachings and his unique response to God's call, we see God present in the world and acting for the world in kind ways.

When centered in God's creative loving kindness we live and move and have our being in a circle of kindness that takes in the whole world. God is in all entities and for all, in the world and for the world. Jesus was responsive to God's love aims and purposes for his life and became more God conscious with each self-actualization.

Jesus' God consciousness, the very real existence of God in Jesus, enabled him to be more conscious of the needs of others in an ever widening circle of loving kindness, and thus more fully divine and human.

Jesus spoke to God as a child would speak to a parent, confidently and securely. Jesus saw God like a kind father and nurturing mother.

> The biblical image of faith in the time of Jesus was of a child wrapped in the folds of a mother's garment where there is security, comfort, nurturing, love, kindness, and hope.

God's loving kindness involves God as present in the world. Responsive love is often suffering love. God suffers with the world. We know from **personal experience** what Isaiah, Hosea, and Jesus learned: that loving kindness is a sympathetic response from one person to another. True kindness feels what the other person is feeling, rejoicing in their joys and hurting with their pains. We would doubt that a husband loves his wife if he were not aware of her feelings and if his feelings did not reflect her feelings and respond with kindness.

As we experience God revealed in the prophets, psalmists, and in Jesus, we find God rejoicing with us in our times of joy and weeping with us in our times of sorrow. Our kindness toward others is based on this responsive kindness we see in God. Our theology should reflect the awe and wonder of God being in the world, in us, and for us, holding us close as a mother wraps her child in the folds of her garments or tenderly holds her child in her lap.

The world does not exist apart from God. God the Gardener loves natural beauty. The Gardener, in tenderness, hovers over every blade of grass and whispers, "Awake. Grow. Grow beautiful and green." Meadows grow, giving way to gurgling streams, water plants, butterflies, hummingbirds, flitting from red, orange, and yellow flowers. Beautiful gardens answer the call and over eons of time, all nature is lured toward ever enriching possibilities until conditions are right for life forms to emerge. Over billions of years God called forth a world able to support human beings.

Humans are a new song that nature hums, the music swells with each new stanza, giving purpose and meaning. Humans moved from being gatherers in the garden to being gardeners, ever singing nature's love songs. Love, kind acts, and doing the right thing---these are all products of the garden within us that we nurture with God's guidance. Sometimes God's kindness can come through the facial expression of our grandchildren, or the touch of a friend when we are hurting. In these special moments the music becomes a joint love song that we sing to God moving us to trust God's guidance and listen to that symphony of voices within that guide us to be kind to one another.

God calls and lures the world forward in tenderness, inspiring novel love aims and goals within all parts of creation. God is supremely socially related with the purpose of sharing goodness and loving kindness with all of creation. God, all nature, and humans are interconnected. As God is immanent in the world, I am in nature and nature is in me. As I write these words I am looking at the snow- capped Chugach Mountains of Alaska wrapped in a rainbow. I am in the mountains and the mountains illumined by rainbows are in me, singing their song, filling every part of my body and spirit with a wealth of beauty. Observing God's beautiful world is a centering experience of tenderness.

The individual as a deciding entity who sings the love songs of nature is not lost in this adventurous process of kindness for all of life is socially related. The God we meet in the beauty of nature and on the pages of the Bible, especially in the tender teachings and actions of Jesus, is in us and for us. The goodness and beauty of the natural world reflects the goodness, grace, beauty, and kindness of God. God is tenderly present in all things.

The call of God toward kindness is nurtured in rainbows and wrapped in a long covenant of love between God and Israel. God supremely revealed in Jesus' tender teachings is a call to all people. (See my book, Gentle Galilean Glories: The Tender Teachings of Jesus). For Christians, Jesus is the supreme example of loving kindness. To affirm this does not lessen the role of Moses for Judaism, Mohammed for Islam or Buddha for Buddhism, and other important religious teachers. Buddha said often, "My religion is kindness." When any one relates to the God of creative possibilities, creative transformation occurs, bringing harmony and peace.

God's loving kindness is persuasive and luring, not coercive and demanding. Relational kindness does not seek to control with coercion. Relational power is greatest in its ability to influence others. If we love someone we do not seek to control or pressure them with promises and threats. Instead we try to persuade them with tender luring love to actualize the possibilities for goodness, beauty, and kindness. The gentle Galilean glories of Jesus define power in terms of loving kindness. power expressed as a power-field of love energies issuing in kindness is transformational. These love energies are seen and experienced in God who relates to us in mysterious ways.

This relational God calls all persons into this power field of love energies that transform persons and God's own self. God is first and foremost transformed by the experience of Jesus' tender life, suffering, death, and resurrection. Through Jesus' deep socially developed God-consciousness, God is revealed to us in new and transforming ways of kindness. This is God's own self-revelation. In these special relationships, God wills to be in us and for us, in the world and for the world.

God as relational kindness is a vision that can change our world into one community knitted together by kind words and gentle loving actions. (For a more complete development of a relational hermeneutic of kindness see my book, A Relational Hermeneutic of Kindness). This hope filled vision taps into the healing energy of kindness found in most religions and makes it the prism through which we understand God, the world, and all things.

Kindness is the language

known around the world.

In many cultures and religions,

rainbows reveal this loving presence of God.

Wrapped in God's rainbow of kindness

we are all one.

Appendix III, Jesus' Kindness Fulfills Rainbow Promises

1. "God's love and **kindness** will shine upon us like the sun that rises in the sky. On us who live in the dark shadow of death, this light will shine to guide us into a life of peace" (Luke 1:78-79).

2. Jesus said, "Come to me, all of you who are tired from carrying heavy loads, and I will give your rest. Take my yoke and put it on you, and learn from me, because I am **gentle and humble in spirit**; and you will find rest. For the yoke I will give you is easy and the load I will put on you is light." (Matthew 11:28-30).

3. Jesus said, "**Blessed are the gentle**, they will receive what God has promised!" (Matthew 5:5).

4. Jesus taught, "People who are well do not need a doctor, but only those who are sick. Go and find out what is meant by the scripture that says, 'It is **kindness** that I want, not animal sacrifices.' I have not come to call respectable people, but outcasts." (Matthew 9:12-13)

5. "A man with leprosy came to Jesus and knelt down. **Jesus felt sorry for him** so he put his hands on him and said, 'You are well.'" (Mark 1:40-41).

6. "Jesus said, "Don't worry about your life. **God will take care of you.**" (Luke 12:22-26).

7. Paul in imitating the spirit of Jesus, grounds kindness in the being of God, "You are God's people so **be gentle, kind, humble, and meek**." (Colossians 3:12).

8. "**Be kind and merciful**, and forgive others, just as God forgave you because of Jesus." (Ephesians 4:32).

9. "I pray that you will **be blessed with kindness** and peace from God, who is and was and is coming. May you receive kindness and peace from Jesus, the faithful witness." (Revelation 1:4-5).

10. "I pray that **Jesus will be kind to all of you**." (Revelation 22:2).

OTHER BOOKS BY DWAYNE COLE

A Center that Holds: Adventures in Kindness
Alpenglow Miracles: Fire Dance of Wonder
A Prayer of Blessing: As You Go Remember This
A Relational Hermeneutic of Kindness
A Relational Trinity of Kindness
BEARS AND MOOSE OF ALASKA: Nature Poetry
Clouds of Inspiration
Down on the Farm in Georgia: A Poetic Memoir
Dragonfly Magic
Gentle Galilean Glories: The Tender Teachings of Jesus
God and Evil: An Ode to Kindness
Heart Haiku: Alaska Inspired Photos and Poems
Heart Sijo: Alaska Inspired Photos and Poems
Jesus' Transforming Beatitudes: Selected Sermons from Year A
Jesus' Transforming Love: Selected Sermons from Year B
Jesus' Transforming Gentle Teachings: Selected Sermons from Year C
Kindness Is Every Step
Lone Leaf Dancing
Poems Inspired by Process Philosophy
Poet of the Universe: A Vision of Beauty and Goodness.
The Apostles' Creed: A Living Creed for the Living Church
The Bible: A Poetic Journey
The Book of Revelation: Jesus' Kindness Transforms Suffering
The Serenity Prayer: A Pathway to Peace and Happiness
The Story of the Bible: Authority, Inspiration, Canonization, and Translation
TREES AND DRIFTWOOD: Poetic Ecology
When Flowers Speak, Listen
WINGS OF INSPIRATION

www.ingramcontent.com/pod-product-compliance
Lightning Source LLC
Chambersburg PA
CBHW051541120626
46551CB00013B/1329